The Medieval World

Famous People
of the Middle Ages

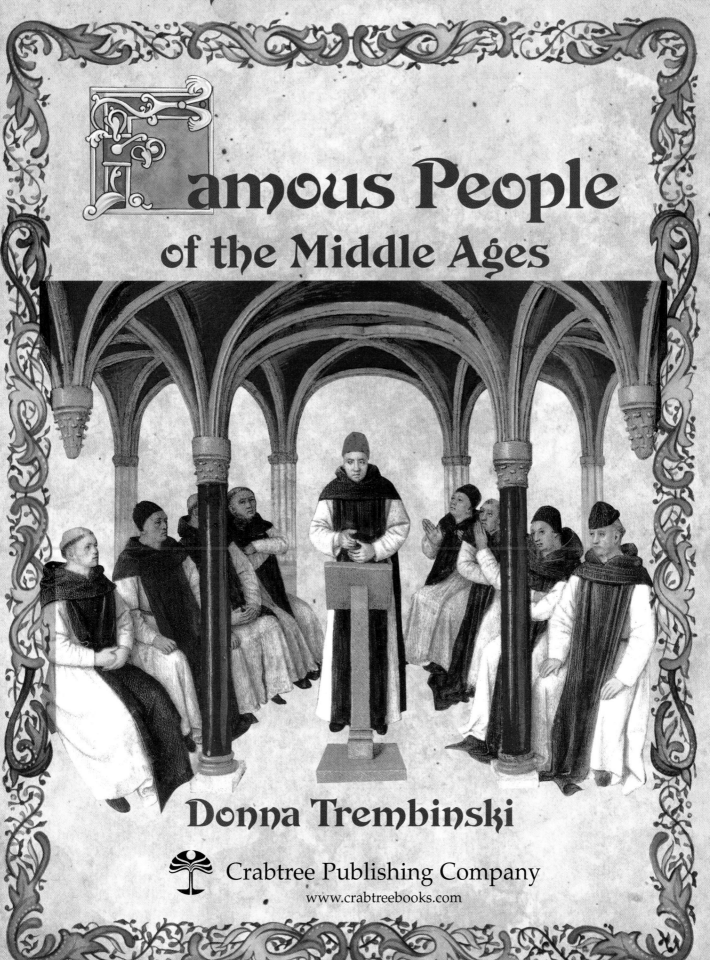

Donna Trembinski

Crabtree Publishing Company
www.crabtreebooks.com

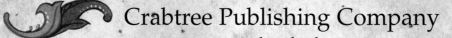

Crabtree Publishing Company

www.crabtreebooks.com

Coordinating editor: Ellen Rodger

Series editor: Carrie Gleason

Project editor: L. Michelle Nielsen

Designer and production coordinator: Rosie Gowsell

Production assistant: Samara Parent

Scanning technician: Arlene Arch-Wilson

Art director: Rob MacGregor

Project development, editing, photo editing, and layout:
First Folio Resource Group, Inc.: Tom Dart, Greg Duhaney, Sarah Gleadow, Debbie Smith

Photo research: Maria DeCambra

Consultant: Isabelle Cochelin, University of Toronto

Photographs: Alinari/Art Resource, NY: p. 25 (bottom); Archivo Iconografico, S.A./Corbis: p. 10; Art Archive/Biblioteca Civica Lucca/Dagli Orti: p. 19 (right); Art Archive/Biblioteca Nazionale Marciana Venice/Dagli Orti: p. 21 (right); Art Archive/Biblioteca Nazionale Turin/Dagli Orti: p. 20; Art Archive/Bibliothèque de l'Arsenal Paris/Marc Charmet: p. 6; Art Archive/British Library: p. 13, p. 22; Art Archive/Monastery of the Rabida, Palos, Spain/Dagli Orti: p. 29; Art Archive/Dagli Orti: p. 8 (right), p. 23; Art Archive/San Francesco Assisi/Dagli Orti: p. 17 (top); Art Archive/Scrovegni Chapel Padua/Dagli Orti: p. 24 (top); Art Archive/University Library Heidelberg/Dagli Orti: p. 5; Art Archive/Victoria and Albert Museum/Graham Brandon: p. 31 (top); Bayerische Staatsbibliothek, Munich/Bridgeman Art

Library: p. 14; Stefano Bianchetti/Corbis: p. 12; Biblioteca Estense, Modena, Italy/Bridgeman Art Library: p. 18; Bibliothèque Nationale, Paris/Bridgeman Art Library: p. 11 (bottom), p. 28; British Library/Bridgeman Art Library: p. 19 (left); British Library/Royal 14.E.IV f.28v: p. 27 (top); Giraudon/Art Resource, NY: title page, p. 9, p. 15, p. 21 (left); Granger Collection, New York: p. 26, p. 31 (bottom); Erich Lessing/Art Resource, NY: p. 7, p. 27 (bottom); Mary Evans/Edwin Wallace: p. 30; Francis G. Mayer/Corbis: p. 24 (bottom); Musée Dobrée, Nantes, France/Bridgeman Art Library: cover; Musée Guimet, Paris, Archives Charmet/Bridgeman Art Library: p. 8 (left); National Gallery of Scotland, Edinburgh/Bridgeman Art Library: p. 17 (bottom); Réunion des Musées Nationaux/Art Resource, NY: p. 16; Scala/Art Resource, NY: p. 11 (top); Jim Zuckerman/Corbis: p. 25 (top)

Map: Samara Parent, Margaret Amy Salter: p. 5

Illustrations: Katherine Kantor: flags, title page (border), copyright page (bottom); Margaret Amy Salter: borders, gold boxes, title page (illuminated letter), copyright page (top), contents page (background), pp. 4-5 (timeline), p. 4 (pyramid), p. 32 (all)

Cover: At age 17, the peasant girl Joan of Arc became one of the most famous teenagers in history after leading a French army to victory over the English at Orléans, in France.

Title page: St. Bernard of Clairvaux was one of the most important religious leaders of the Middle Ages. He preached during the Second Crusade, advised popes and kings, and founded many new monasteries.

Crabtree Publishing Company

www.crabtreebooks.com   1-800-387-7650

In Canada: We acknowledge the financial support of the Government of Canada through the Book Publishing Industry Development Program (BPIDP) for our publishing activities.

Cataloging-in-Publication Data
Trembinski, Donna, 1974-
 The medieval world: famous people of the Middle Ages/
  written by Donna Trembinski.
   p. cm. -- (The medieval world)
Includes index.
ISBN-13: 978-0-7787-1356-2 (RLB)
ISBN-10: 0-7787-1356-3 (RLB)
ISBN-13: 978-0-7787-1388-3 (pbk)
ISBN-10: 0-7787-1388-1 (pbk)
  1. Biography--Middle Ages, 500-1500--Juvenile literature.
  2. Middle Ages--History--Juvenile literature. I. Title.

CT114.T74 2005
920'.009'02--dc22   2005019026
                                                                  LC

**Published in
the United States**
PMB 16A
350 Fifth Ave.
Suite 3308
New York, NY
10118

**Published
in Canada**
616 Welland Ave.
St. Catharines
Ontario, Canada
L2M 5V6

**Published in the
United Kingdom**
73 Lime Walk
Headington
Oxford
OX3 7AD
United Kingdom

**Published
in Australia**
386 Mt. Alexander Rd.
Ascot Vale (Melbourne)
VIC 3032

Table of Contents

Medieval Fame

In western Europe, the time between 500 A.D. and 1500 was known as the Middle Ages, or the medieval period. Society was divided into four main parts. Peasants farmed the land. Townspeople worked in different trades, such as making shoes, baking bread, and selling household goods. Priests, monks, and nuns devoted their lives to God. Lords, such as kings and great nobles, ruled over the people.

Winning Fame

Certain medieval people became well known for their actions and accomplishments. Kings and queens became famous for conquering, or taking by force, new territories, defending those they ruled, and passing laws that protected the people on their lands. Inventors were praised for their creations, and explorers were celebrated for discovering parts of the world previously unknown to Europeans. Even people who broke the law gained fame, but for their bad deeds and not their good ones.

▼ *In the Middle Ages, lords owned most of the land and wealth, but 90 percent of the population were peasants. Most peasants had to work on a lord's land, producing food to feed the lord's household.*

The prophet Muhammad claims to hear messages from God and begins to teach the new religion of Islam
610

Viking explorer Leif Eriksson arrives in North America
1001

Chinese inventor Su Sung builds a very accurate water clock
1092

Italian philosopher Thomas Aquinas begins writing *Summary of Theology*
1265

Wat Tyler leads the Peasants' Rebellion in England
1381

980
Erik the Red kills two men and is banished from his home in Iceland

1066
William the Conqueror wins the Battle of Hastings and becomes king of England

1187
Kurdish warrior Saladin captures the city of Jerusalem

1307
Dante Alighieri begins writing *The Divine Comedy*

▲ *Famous rulers, warriors, inventors, painters, and writers came from many different places in the Middle Ages. News of their accomplishments was spread throughout the medieval world by storytellers, explorers, and other travelers.*

Spreading the Word

News of people's achievements, both good and bad, was spread by word of mouth. Professional storytellers called minstrels traveled from place to place, telling stories in nobles' homes and in market squares.

Not every inventor, artist, or writer in the Middle Ages became famous. Many who constructed great buildings, painted beautiful pictures, or wrote wonderful poetry did not sign their names to their work. Over time, the names were forgotten or lost, but many of the works they left behind added to the rich culture of the medieval world.

▼ *Minstrels often played music on instruments such as lutes and recorders, which added drama to their stories.*

Architect Filippo Brunelleschi completes the dome of the Florence Cathedral in Italy

1436

1431
Joan of Arc is burned at the stake for heresy

1492
Isabella I, queen of Castile, sponsors Christopher Columbus' first voyage across the Atlantic Ocean

Powerful Kings

Medieval kings led knights to war, founded cities and empires, and governed people under their rule, called subjects. Not all kings were successful rulers. Some lost many wars and a great deal of territory, while others became unpopular for claiming too much power and forcing people to pay very high taxes.

Justinian I (483 A.D.–565 A.D.)

Justinian I became the emperor of **Byzantium** in 527 A.D. One of his greatest accomplishments was collecting and organizing the laws of Byzantium into what became known as the Justinian Code. The Justinian Code contained laws that protected property, outlined the rights of women, and made offenses such as murder and assault illegal. It was used as the basis for the justice system, or law-keeping, in Byzantium for the next thousand years. It also became one of the bases of law in western Europe.

Charlemagne (ca. 742 A.D.–814 A.D.)

Charlemagne was king of the Franks, a people who had migrated from present-day Germany and Poland to the area that is now France, Belgium, and western Germany. Charlemagne, whose name means "Charles the Great," fought many battles and conquered many lands. At the time, his empire was the largest in Europe. The lands under his rule became great centers of culture and learning. Charlemagne encouraged monks to teach reading and writing to young nobles, and founded a school at his palace in Aachen, Germany.

▲ *Charlemagne conquered lands and promoted the Christian religion in the territories he ruled. As a reward, Pope Leo III crowned him emperor on Christmas Day, 800 A.D.*

ET HIC EPISCOPVS CIBV ET POTV BE NE DIC IT O

▲ *The story of the Battle of Hastings is told in an embroidered wall hanging known as the Bayeux Tapestry. Here, William and his men celebrate their successful crossing to England with a great feast.*

William the Conqueror (1028–1087)

In 1066, King Edward of England died, and his brother-in-law, Harold, became king. William of Normandy, who controlled an area in what is now northern France, was determined to win the English throne. With around 600 ships of soldiers, servants, and horses, William set sail for southern England.

The Battle of Hastings was fought on October 14, 1066. William's soldiers were better armed and better rested than Harold's men, who had just finished fighting in northeastern England. The Normans defeated Harold's army, and Harold was killed. William, who became known as William the Conqueror, was crowned the new king of England.

Sundjata (ca. 1215–1255)

Great empires also existed in medieval Africa. Sundjata, whose name means "Lion Lord," founded the Malian Empire of medieval Africa. At its most powerful, the empire stretched from the Atlantic Ocean to the Sahara Desert in Africa. In creating his empire, Sundjata brought together the tribes of northwestern Africa, established a new capital, and founded cities that were protected by high walls and armies. He helped the region become wealthy by encouraging his tribes to trade gold and salt with peoples from northern Africa and western Asia. Even though Sundjata was a king, he lived as a farmer, which was considered a noble occupation for members of his tribe.

Women Rule

Many medieval queens ruled lands, governed peoples, and fought wars, just as kings did. Queens often stayed in power only until their sons were old enough to become kings. In a few instances, a queen liked ruling so much that she refused to give up the throne.

Theodora (ca. 500 A.D.–548 A.D.) ▶

Theodora, the wife of Emperor Justinian I, was one of the most powerful women in the Byzantine Empire. She was among Justinian's most trusted advisors. Advisors were people who helped the king. Theodora handled political matters with such skill that some people mistook her for the ruler of Byzantium. She met with government officials from other countries and used her influence to support issues that were important to her. Among these issues was ensuring that people had the freedom to marry whomever they wished, regardless of **social class**.

◀ Wu Zetian (625 A.D.–705 A.D.)

Wu Zetian ruled the Chinese Empire alongside her husband, Emperor Kao-Tsung. When Kao-Tsung became ill, Wu Zetian took over his duties. As empress, she did not tolerate any opposition, and dismissed, **exiled**, or even killed those who did not support her.

When Kao-Tsung died, Wu Zetian named her second son emperor, but she remained the real force behind the throne. Finally, she seized power from her son and governed alone for the next 15 years as the only female emperor in Chinese history.

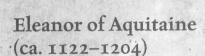

Eleanor of Aquitaine (ca. 1122–1204)

Eleanor was the ruler of Aquitaine, an area in what is now southern France. At age 15, she **inherited** the land from her father. Eleanor continued to control Aquitaine after marrying Louis VII, who became king of France.

Eleanor and Louis were not happily married, and their marriage was annulled, or ended, by the **Catholic Church**. Eleanor then married Henry II, who became king of England. She helped her husband govern, and later, two of her sons, Richard the Lionheart and John I. She governed in place of Richard while he was on **crusade**, and she defended John from a challenge to his throne.

Isabella I (1451–1504) ▼

Together, Isabella I and her husband, Ferdinand II, controlled most of Spain in the late 1400s. As queen, Isabella led wars, including a successful attack against **Muslims** ruling Granada, a kingdom in southern Spain. She and Ferdinand created the Spanish Inquisition, a court that punished heretics, or people accused of holding beliefs that went against the Catholic Church's teachings.

Isabella also funded schools and the arts, and sponsored explorers, including Christopher Columbus. As Columbus' **patron**, Isabella became queen of all the lands that he conquered.

Famous Fighters

Knights were warriors who fought on horseback with long swords or axes. They went to war for their lords, who wanted to gain more territory and power. They also fought to protect their land and the peasants who worked on it.

Charles Martel (ca. 688 A.D.–741 A.D.)

Charles Martel, whose name means "Charles the Hammer," was born in what is now Belgium. By 719 A.D., he had become second in command to the Frankish king, Chilperic II. Chilperic was king in name only. Charles was the true ruler.

Charles fought many battles, including the Battle of Poitiers, also known as the Battle of Tours, in 733 A.D. His soldiers fought Muslim warriors who were raiding villages in western France. The Muslim leader was killed on the first day, and his army fled during the night. Charles declared himself the winner, and the Muslims' attempt to conquer land in France came to an end.

Saladin (ca. 1137–1193)

Saladin was one of the best-known Muslim warriors of the Middle Ages. Born in Mesopotamia, in present-day Iraq, he led many successful battles against **Christian** warriors called crusaders, and eventually ruled over large parts of the **Middle East**.

One of Saladin's greatest victories was on July 4, 1187, at the Battle of Hattin. His army defeated the crusaders by trapping them between two large hills, called the Horns of Hattin. Three months later, Saladin took back the holy city of Jerusalem, which had been in European hands for nearly a hundred years.

▲ *At the Battle of Poitiers, most of Charles Martel's army fought on foot, using axes, swords, daggers, and lances, which are long poles with sharp points. The Muslim soldiers fought on horseback with swords and lances.*

Crusades

The crusades were a series of wars fought for almost 200 years in present-day Israel, Jordan, and Syria, particularly around the city of Jerusalem. Jews, Muslims, and Christians all consider this area holy. The First Crusade was launched in 1096 by Christian warriors who were determined to gain control of the area, then in Muslim hands. At first, the crusaders were successful, setting up Christian kingdoms in the region, but none of the kingdoms lasted more than 300 years.

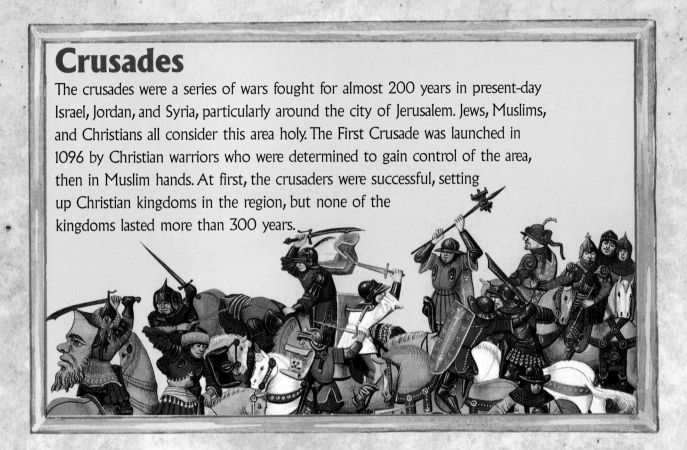

Genghis Khan (ca. 1155–1227)

Genghis Khan, whose name means "universal ruler," was a fierce warrior who lived in present-day Mongolia. He won many battles that allowed him to unite, or bring together, the Mongol tribes and extend his empire across Asia.

Genghis Khan's knowledge of military strategy made him very successful in battle. He used hundreds of thousands of warriors mounted on horseback to capture other Mongol tribes on the battlefield, and siege warfare to take control of entire cities. In a siege, the attacking army surrounded the enemy's city walls so that no people or supplies could get in or out. Attackers smashed city gates with battering rams, and flung rocks and flaming garbage over the walls with large slingshot-like machines called catapults. The siege ended when people in the city either gave up or starved to death.

▲ *The territory Genghis Khan ruled was so vast that it was said to take two years to cross it on horseback.*

Heroic Peasants

In the Middle Ages, peasants, most of whom could not read or write, did not keep a record of their achievements. Still, some peasants' names and deeds have survived. Some became skilled writers and artists, while others became strong leaders, fighting for a better life for themselves and others.

William Tell (1300s)

William Tell is a legendary peasant hero. He is said to have lived in present-day Switzerland at a time when it was ruled by emperors from present-day Germany and Austria.

One day in town, William refused to bow before a hat in the market square that represented the emperor, Albert I. The local **bailiff**, who thought William was being disrespectful, offered him a choice: he either had to bow or shoot an apple off the head of his own son. William chose to shoot, and sent an arrow straight through the apple.

The bailiff congratulated William, then asked him why he had an extra arrow. William replied, "To kill you, if I had killed my son by accident." William was arrested and taken by boat to the governor's castle, but he escaped during a storm. Hiding in the rocks just outside the castle, he waited for the bailiff and killed him when he came ashore.

▼ *William broke free from his captors and regained his freedom. The story of William Tell is probably not true, but it inspired the Swiss to fight for independence from their German and Austrian rulers.*

Wat Tyler (ca. 1340–1381)

Wat Tyler was one of the leaders of the Peasants' Rebellion, which broke out in England in 1381. Peasants were angry that they were earning poor wages, paying high taxes, and being forced to fight in a war against France.

On June 7, Tyler led a large group of peasant soldiers to the city of Canterbury. There, they demolished the **archbishop**'s castle and freed prisoners from the local prison.

Five days later, Tyler's rebels joined other rebels in London. King Richard II, fearing violence, agreed to some of the peasants' demands. Unfortunately, many rebels had already begun destroying the city and beheading, or cutting off the heads of, royal officials.

On June 15, Tyler met with King Richard to stop the violence, but was stabbed by the mayor of London during the meeting. Having lost their leader, the rebels gave up. The freedoms that the king had granted were taken back soon after Tyler's death.

Jacques (ca. 1358)

French nobles nicknamed peasants "Jacques." The word Jacquerie, used to refer to a French peasant revolt that took place in 1358, comes from this nickname.

French peasants rebelled because they were forced to pay high taxes to fund a war with England. They also had to work much harder after a deadly **plague**, called the Black Death, swept through Europe, leaving fewer peasants to do the same amount of work.

During the Jacquerie rebellion, peasants burned down the houses of their lords and killed entire families of nobles. The nobles fought back, killing thousands of peasants and putting an end to the revolt.

▲ *The peasant rebels of the Jacquerie were poorly equipped to fight against nobles and knights, who could afford swords and armor.*

Children in Charge

Some children in the Middle Ages helped their families in the fields, served nobles in their castles, and learned trades. Others became famous kings, warriors, and religious leaders.

Otto III (980 A.D.–1002 A.D.) ▶

Otto III was named king of Germany and Italy at the age of three. Unfortunately, his **guardian**, Henry the Quarrelsome, wanted to be king and decided to keep young Otto imprisoned so he would not be able to rule. Eventually, the Church forced Henry to release Otto into the care of his mother and grandmother. They acted as his regents, ruling in Otto's place until he was 14, at which time he began serving as king and emperor. In 998 A.D., Otto settled in Rome, in present-day Italy. He was forced to flee three years later when the Romans grew unhappy and rebelled. He died at the age of 22, while planning an attack on Rome.

Baldwin IV — The Leper King (ca. 1161–1185)

Baldwin IV's grandfather and father were Christian kings who ruled the city of Jerusalem. When his father, Amalric I, died in 1174, Baldwin became king. He was only 13 years old.

Baldwin was a fierce warrior, in spite of the fact that he was young and suffered from leprosy, a disease that weakens the body. In 1177, Baldwin and his army easily defeated the powerful Muslim warrior Saladin, who was trying to capture Jerusalem. Saladin had underestimated his young enemy. It was only after Baldwin died of leprosy at the age of 24 that Saladin captured the holy city.

Joan of Arc (1412–1431)

Joan was a peasant girl from northwestern France. Around the age of 12, she claimed to hear the voices of saints, or holy people believed to able to talk to God. The voices told her that she would help save France from the English during the Hundred Years War. Five years later, Joan convinced Charles of Ponthieu, the heir, or next in line, to the French throne, to let her lead French troops against the English. The English were trying to capture the French city of Orléans. Charles made Joan a knight, gave her permission to dress as a soldier, and sent her to Orléans with an army. Under her leadership, the French troops won the battle at Orléans. The war did not go in France's favor for long. In 1430, a small party of French troops led by Joan was defeated in northern France, and Joan was captured. Charles, now King Charles VII, did not attempt to rescue Joan. She was tried for heresy and witchcraft because of her claim to hear saints' voices and for continuing to dress as a man. Joan was sentenced to death. On May 30, 1431, at the age of 19, she was burned at the stake.

▼ *Twenty-five years after Joan of Arc was burned at the stake, the Church overturned, or reversed, the verdict of heresy. In 1920, the Church declared Joan a saint. Today, she is a patron saint, or protector, of France.*

Religious Leaders

People who developed new ideas about religion were among the most famous medieval leaders. Some Christians who led very holy lives were declared saints by the Church. Like today, people prayed to saints for protection and good health.

Saint Benedict of Nursia (ca. 480 A.D.–547 A.D.)

Born in Nursia, Italy, Saint Benedict founded a monastery in Monte Cassino, Italy. Monasteries are communities where monks and nuns live. Monks in the monastery followed Benedict's instructions on how to live. The instructions Benedict gave became known as the Benedictine Rule. The Rule asked that monks be obedient to God. It described when and how monks should pray, study, work, eat, bathe, dress, and sleep. The Benedictine Rule was adopted by many monasteries across Europe, and is still followed in some monasteries today.

Muhammad (ca. 570 A.D.–632 A.D.)

Muhammad was from the Middle East. He was the founder of Islam, one of the world's main religions. In 610 A.D., Muhammad claimed to receive a message from the angel Gabriel telling him that he would be God's, or Allah's, **prophet**. Gabriel taught Muhammad Allah's lessons about how to lead a good life, and told him to spread these teachings to others. At first, many people rejected Muhammad's teachings and threatened to kill him, but by the time Muhammad died in 632 A.D., Islam was spreading. Over the next 200 years, Islam became the major religion of many regions, including western Asia, northern Africa, and Spain.

◀ *In this illustration from the book* **Siyar-i Nabi,** *or* **The Life of the Prophet,** *the angel Gabriel reveals Allah's teachings to Muhammad.*

Saint Francis of Assisi (ca. 1182–1226)

Saint Francis of Assisi was born in Italy, the son of a wealthy **merchant**. When he was in his early twenties, he had a **vision** that inspired him to devote his life to God. He and his followers founded the Franciscan Order of friars in 1209. Friars, unlike monks, did not live apart from other people. They lived in towns, where they spread God's teachings and helped the poor and sick. The Franciscan Order grew to include thousands and, in 1212, Francis established an order for women that came to be known as the Poor Clares.

▲ *Francis preached to animals, as well as to people. Today, Francis is the patron saint of animals and the environment, and is one of Italy's patron saints.*

◀ Saint Catherine of Siena (1347–1380)

Saint Catherine was born in Siena, Italy. At the age of six or seven, she saw her first vision of Jesus Christ, who Christians believe is God's son. Hoping to see more visions, Catherine began spending almost all of her time alone. She rarely left her bedroom, where she prayed constantly.

At the age of 23, Catherine claimed to have received a message from God telling her to rejoin public life. She began to nurse the sick, help the poor, and write letters of advice to kings, queens, and the Pope. Many people began to flock to her, drawn by her knowledge of God's teachings. In 1377, Catherine wrote *The Book*. *The Book*, now known as *The Dialogue of St. Catherine of Siena*, was a guide for how to lead a religious life. Catherine was named one of Italy's patron saints in 1461.

Great Scholars

The first great European schools were founded in the 1000s and 1100s. People at these schools, called scholars, studied subjects such as music, mathematics, and logic. Logic is the study of reasoning, or thought. The new ways in which scholars looked at these topics strongly influenced other people's thinking.

Avicenna
(ca. 980 A.D.–1037 A.D.)

Avicenna, or Ibn Sina in Arabic, was one of the greatest thinkers of the medieval world. He was a physician, **philosopher**, and scientist. Avicenna was born in Bukhara, Iran, which was a center of Muslim learning. Avicenna was educated by his father and the many philosophers and tutors, or teachers, who visited his home.

One of Avicenna's most important teachers was a grocer who taught him about herbs that could be used as medicine. By age 16, Avicenna was a well-known healer. He became the personal physician of the prince, then worked for the government. At night, he wrote books about logic, physics, mathematics, and medicine. The most famous of his 300 works include the *Book of Healing*, a five-volume medical encyclopedia, and the *Canon of Medicine*, about various illnesses and their treatments. Many of Avicenna's works were later taught in the universities of western Europe.

▲ *This page, which shows an apothecary's shop, appears in the* Canon of Medicine. *The* Canon of Medicine *was used for centuries by doctors and scholars in Europe and the Middle East.*

Hildegard of Bingen (1098–1179)

Hildegard was a German nun who became the abbess, or leader, of a monastery she founded near the city of Bingen. She advised popes and kings about religious matters, and wrote about her visions, which she began experiencing at a young age. Hildegard composed musical plays that praised God and taught the nuns of her monastery to lead holy lives. She is one of the only women from the Middle Ages known to have written music for church services. Hildegard was also known for her books about medicine and science. These books were used by healers and physicians until the end of the Middle Ages.

▶ *This illustration from Hildegard of Bingen's* **The Book of Divine Works** *shows one of her visions, in which people pray and build churches.*

◀ Thomas Aquinas (1225–1274)

Thomas Aquinas is considered the greatest religious thinker and philosopher of the Catholic Church. Born in Italy to a noble family who wanted him to become a Benedictine monk, Thomas became a friar instead and dedicated his life to preaching in the towns of Italy. He studied theology, science, philosophy, and logic at the University of Paris. Eventually, he became a teacher of theology. In his greatest work, the *Summa theologiae*, or *Summary of Theology*, Thomas used logic to prove that God existed. Thomas died before completing the *Summa theologiae*.

Writers

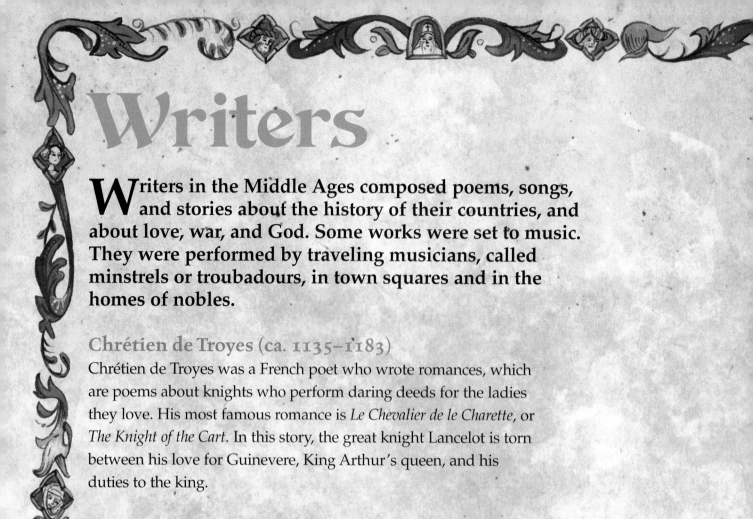

Writers in the Middle Ages composed poems, songs, and stories about the history of their countries, and about love, war, and God. Some works were set to music. They were performed by traveling musicians, called minstrels or troubadours, in town squares and in the homes of nobles.

Chrétien de Troyes (ca. 1135–1183)

Chrétien de Troyes was a French poet who wrote romances, which are poems about knights who perform daring deeds for the ladies they love. His most famous romance is *Le Chevalier de le Charette*, or *The Knight of the Cart*. In this story, the great knight Lancelot is torn between his love for Guinevere, King Arthur's queen, and his duties to the king.

Chrétien de Troyes also wrote *Perceval*, the story of a knight in search of a holy object called the Grail. He left this romance unfinished, but the characters he introduced were so popular that other authors soon began to write about them. Even today, authors write new versions of the legends of King Arthur's knights and the quest for the Grail.

▶ *Chrétien de Troyes wrote stories about many of King Arthur's Knights of the Round Table, including Lancelot, Perceval, and Gawain.*

Dante is led through Heaven by Beatrice, his one true love.

Dante Alighieri (1265–1321)

Dante Alighieri was an Italian poet and writer. His long poem, *La Divina Commedia*, or *The Divine Comedy*, is considered one of the great pieces of literature.

In *La Divina Commedia*, Dante is guided on a journey through Hell and **Purgatory** before he is led to Heaven. Deep underground, in Hell, he witnesses people being chewed in the mouths of great beasts, pushing heavy rocks, being chased by wild dogs, and receiving other punishments for their sins. On the mountain of Purgatory, Dante sees people seeking forgiveness for their sins so that they may enter Heaven. Finally, on a tour of Heaven, Dante meets angels and saints.

Hafiz (ca. 1320–1390)

Shams al-Din Muhammad, also called Hafiz, is one of the most famous Iranian poets. As a young child, he entertained his family by reciting the poems of great Iranian writers. Their works inspired Hafiz to write poems that told of love, religion, and the city of his birth, Shiraz. The ruler of Shiraz was so enchanted by Hafiz' writings that he hired the poet to entertain him at the royal court. Hafiz' fame grew, and his poems came to be recited throughout the Muslim world, from Turkey to India. *Diwan-i-Hafiz* is a collection of Hafiz' poetry, and remains one of the greatest pieces of medieval literature.

Beautiful illustrations decorate Hafiz' poems about friends who gather together in gardens to listen to music, eat tasty foods, and drink wine.

Geoffrey Chaucer (ca. 1340–1400)

Geoffrey Chaucer was one of the greatest English poets of the Middle Ages. His most famous work, a long poem called *The Canterbury Tales*, tells of a group of **pilgrims** who journey from London to Canterbury. Along the way, they tell each other stories, including one called the "Knight's Tale."

In the "Knight's Tale," two young knights, Arcite and Palamon, are captured by King Theseus and fall in love with his sister-in-law Emily. The king arranges a tournament, or mock battle, in which the two knights compete for Emily. Arcite wins, but soon after is thrown from his horse and dies. Palamon and Emily marry instead.

Christine de Pizan (1364–1430)

Christine de Pizan was a poet and author, one of the few women in the Middle Ages to earn a living from writing. Born in Italy, Christine moved to France at the age of four. She was well educated, and turned to writing when she was 24 to support herself and her three children after her husband's death.

Christine de Pizan's first poems describe the grief she felt at the loss of her husband. Her later writings, which include *The Book of the City of Ladies* and *The Treasury of the City of Ladies*, describe the many contributions women made to medieval society.

▲ *Like other travelers on pilgrimages, the characters in* **The Canterbury Tales** *tell stories, sing songs, and exchange news to pass the time during the long journey.*

Artists at Work

Much of the artwork created in the Middle Ages, from paintings on church walls to beautifully decorated books, was based on religion. Religious works helped people learn stories from the Bible and from the lives of saints.

▲ *The use of exterior supports, called flying buttresses, and pointed arches allowed Gothic cathedrals, such as Saint-Denis, to be taller and more spacious than earlier medieval churches.*

Many great medieval buildings were also created for religious purposes. Often, the only stone building in a village was the church, whose tall spires, or steeples, travelers saw first when they came into a town.

Abbé Suger (1098–1151)

Abbé Suger was a Benedictine monk who became the **abbot** of Saint-Denis, an **abbey** in France. The abbey housed the relics, or sacred remains, of French saints and the graves of many French kings.

To show how important the church was, Suger decided to redesign it in a style that become known as Gothic. He replaced the thick columns and walls of earlier churches, with pointed arches and tall, thin columns to create a more spacious interior. The large stained glass windows that he added allowed more sunlight to enter the church and made it feel, as Suger described it, like Heaven on earth.

At the Capella Scrovegni, a chapel in Padua, Italy, Giotto painted 23 frescoes that depict the life of Jesus Christ. Giotto was known for painting in a more realistic style than other painters of the time.

Giotto (ca. 1266–1337)

Giotto was an Italian **master** painter and **architect**. As a young boy, he served as an **apprentice** to the great artist Cimabue. In time, Giotto learned all he could from Cimabue and began to paint works that were more beautiful than those of his famous master. Giotto is best known for his church frescoes, or paintings on plaster walls, of stories from the Bible and from the life of Saint Francis.

Jean Pucelle (ca. 1300–1334)

The French artist Jean Pucelle was a master illuminator. Illuminators were artists who decorated medieval manuscripts, or books. They used paints made from minerals such as copper, from fruits such as buckthorn berries, and even from dried insects. Pucelle painted illuminations of religious scenes and decorated the borders with leaves and trees.

Jean Pucelle's most famous work is the tiny, beautifully decorated Book of Hours that he created for Jeanne d'Evreux, the queen of France.

Jean Pucelle's illuminations were so popular that members of the French royal family hired him to illustrate their personal Bibles and Books of Hours. Books of Hours contained daily prayers and stories about saints.

Filippo Brunelleschi (1377–1446)

Filippo Brunelleschi began his career as a goldsmith and artist in Florence, Italy. He then became an architect, inspired by beautiful ancient palaces and temples that he saw in Rome.

Brunelleschi's greatest accomplishment was the cupola, or dome, of the cathedral in Florence. The dome is supported by a framework of 24 curved vertical ribs made of stone and marble. The ribs are held in place by horizontal bands of stone, wood, and iron chains, all of which are covered with bricks. The ribs hold the dome so well that it does not require additional support from below.

Leonardo da Vinci (1452–1519)

Leonardo da Vinci was one of the greatest painters of all time, even though he completed fewer than 20 works. Da Vinci was born in a small village near Florence, Italy. He was an apprentice to a master painter at the age of 18, but quickly became more skilled than his teacher.

At age 30, da Vinci went to Milan, Italy, to work. Among his works from this time is *The Last Supper*, a painting that shows Jesus' final meal with his disciples, or followers, before he was crucified, or put to death on a cross. After 18 years in Milan, da Vinci returned to Florence, where he painted his most famous work. His portrait of a wealthy Florentine lady, Lisa del Giocondo, is known as the *Mona Lisa*.

▼ Leonardo da Vinci painted **The Last Supper** *on the walls of the refectory, or dining hall, of the Santa Maria delle Grazie monastery, in Milan, Italy.*

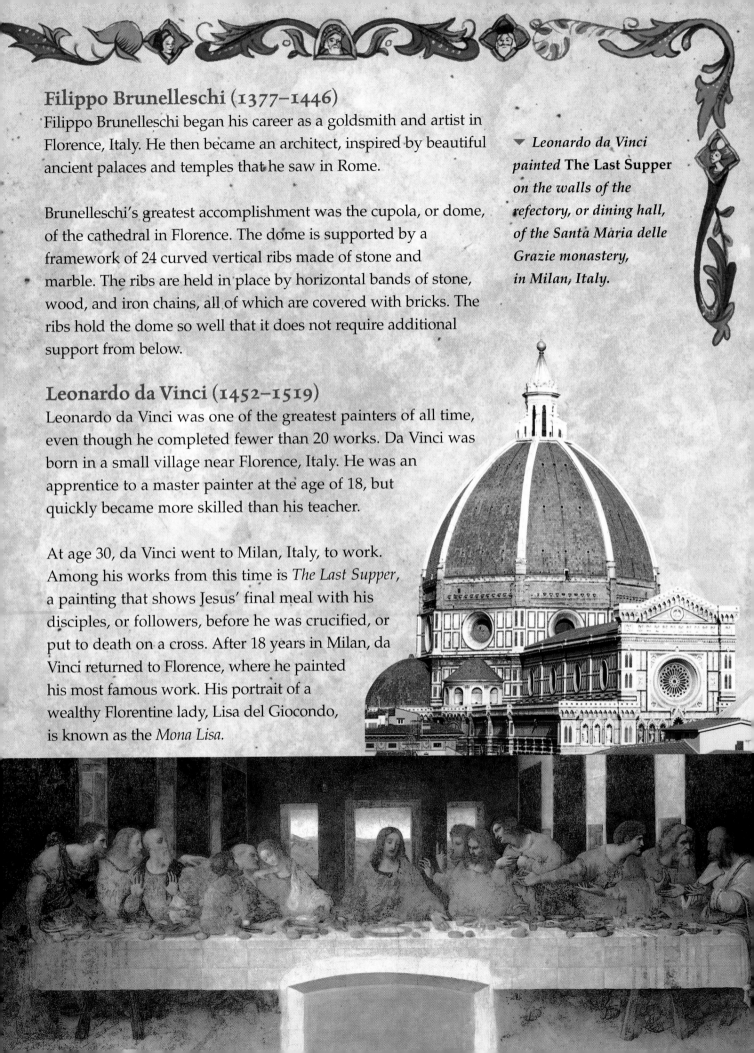

Inventors

Many objects used today were invented in the Middle Ages, including accurate clocks, eyeglasses, microscopes, and the printing press. These inventions changed people's lives by making their work easier and faster.

Su Sung (1020–1101)

In the Middle Ages, people in Asia, Europe, and Africa used water clocks to tell the time. Water clocks are filled with water, which is allowed to escape at a slow speed. Time is measured according to how long it takes the water to escape.

Around 1092, a Chinese inventor named Su Sung built a 30-foot- (12-meter-) high water clock that told time much more accurately than earlier water clocks. It had a mechanism that made the water escape at a constant rate, so the clock was never too fast or too slow. The clock also allowed people to measure the location of the sun, moon, and stars.

Roger Bacon (ca. 1214–1292)

Born in England, Roger Bacon became famous for his scientific research and inventions, which included a magnifying glass and an early version of the microscope. He also studied alchemy, which was both a medieval philosophy and a science. Alchemists believed that they could turn metals, such as lead, into gold, and find the elixir of life, a potion that would keep them young forever. Many people in the Middle Ages considered alchemy witchcraft, and Bacon was imprisoned for his work.

▼ *The Chinese emperor Zhezong considered Su Sung's water clock the greatest mechanical achievement of the time.*

Gunpowder

Roger Bacon was the first European to record instructions for making gunpowder, a Chinese invention. Bacon considered the information so dangerous that he wrote it down in code.

At first, the Chinese used gunpowder only to create fireworks. It was not until 1126 that they used gunpowder in battle. They placed it in bamboo guns that shot bamboo spears, and used it to make bombs that were flung over city walls. These weapons were far more effective than ordinary spears and swords. By the late 1300s, Europeans were fighting with guns, cannon, and cannon balls, which were packed with gunpowder.

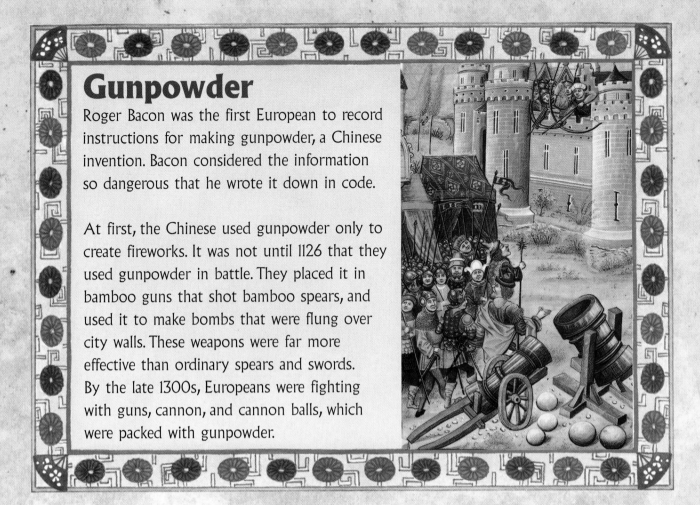

Johannes Gutenberg (ca. 1395–1468)

For most of the Middle Ages, scribes copied and decorated books by hand. Their work was very time consuming and required a great deal of care. As a result, books were very expensive and few people could afford them, so most people did not learn how to read.

This changed when a German jeweler and mirror-maker named Johannes Gutenberg invented the first moveable-type printing press in Europe. He carved letters and punctuation marks into small blocks of wood or lead. Then, he arranged the blocks into words and sentences on a metal plate to make a page of type. Ink was spread over the letters, and a piece of paper was placed on top of them. A firm downward pressure was applied by a machine called a screw-press, and the inked type was transferred to the paper. Many copies of the same page were printed this way. To make a new page, the blocks were rearranged on the metal plate.

▼ Johannes Gutenberg used the printing press to print copies of the Bible, school books, pamphlets, and poems.

Explorers

People in the Middle Ages knew far less about the geography of the world than we do today, and it took great courage to set out into the unknown. Many medieval explorers were brave enough to search for new trade routes, conquer lands for their kings and queens, and seek out new adventures.

Leif Eriksson (1000s)

Leif Eriksson, a **Viking**, was one of the first Europeans to set foot in North America. He set out from Greenland, and landed on an island that he named Helluland. The name for the area, now believed to be Baffin Island, means "Slab Land" or "Flat Rock Land."

From Helluland, Eriksson sailed south to a land of white beaches and trees. He called this land Markland, meaning "Woodland." Today, Markland is believed to be the northern coast of Labrador, in Canada. Continuing farther south, Eriksson found a region with wild grapes, rich forests, and huge salmon swimming in the waters. He named the area Vinland, meaning "Wineland" or "Pastureland." Vinland is believed to be in northern Newfoundland, Canada.

Marco Polo (ca. 1254–1324)

Italian merchant and adventurer Marco Polo traveled with his father and uncle throughout the lands ruled by Kublai Khan, the leader of the Mongol Empire in China. They reported to the great ruler everything they discovered.

The Polos visited cities larger than any European city, tasted wine made from rice instead of grapes, and saw treasures made of a fine ceramic called porcelain and a mineral called jade. After 17 years, they finally decided to return to Italy. Marco wrote about his travels in his book *Divisiament duo monde*, or *Description of the World*.

▼ *When Marco Polo and his father arrived at the court of Kublai Khan, they delivered gifts and letters from the Pope to the Mongol ruler.*

Ibn Battuta (ca. 1304–1377)

Ibn Battuta was the greatest Muslim traveler of the Middle Ages. Born in present-day Morocco, he journeyed to such places as Egypt, Saudi Arabia, Turkey, Afghanistan, India, and Mali, in western Africa. He saw many amazing sights along the way, from the pyramids of Egypt to the elegant palaces of Mali, and he survived many dangers. Ibn Battuta was shipwrecked, attacked by robbers, and almost beheaded by an Indian king. When Ibn Battuta finally finished traveling after 29 years, he had covered around 75,000 miles (120,000 kilometers) and visited 44 countries, including most Muslim lands.

Christopher Columbus (1451–1506)

Christopher Columbus was an Italian explorer, whose four trips across the Atlantic led Europeans to settle in the Americas. In 1492, he convinced the Spanish queen, Isabella I, and her husband, Ferdinand II, to fund an expedition west, into the unknown reaches of the Atlantic. He hoped to find a new trade route to Asia, where many valuable spices were found.

Instead, Columbus landed in the Americas, where he found gold and spices that he brought back to the Spanish queen and king. Isabella and Ferdinand sponsored three more voyages in the hope of finding further riches. Columbus never found gold like that from his first journey, nor did he find a route to Asia.

▼ *Christopher Columbus believed that he could reach Asia faster by sailing west than by traveling east over land. He was disappointed that he never found a western route to Asia.*

Criminals

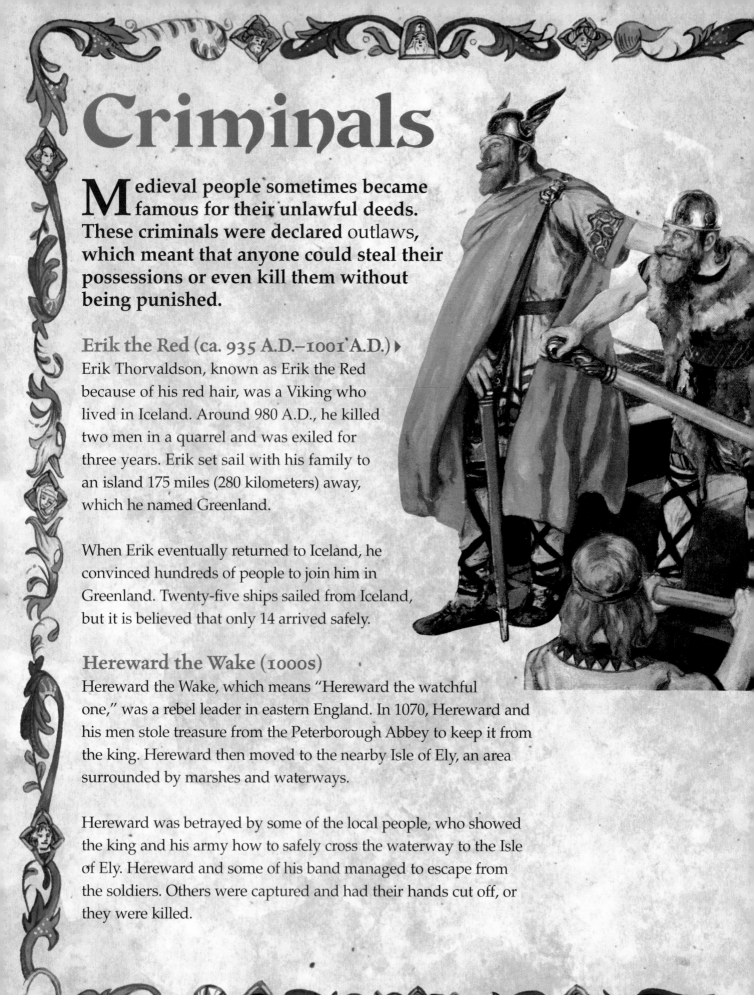

Medieval people sometimes became famous for their unlawful deeds. These criminals were declared outlaws, which meant that anyone could steal their possessions or even kill them without being punished.

Erik the Red (ca. 935 A.D.–1001 A.D.) ▶

Erik Thorvaldson, known as Erik the Red because of his red hair, was a Viking who lived in Iceland. Around 980 A.D., he killed two men in a quarrel and was exiled for three years. Erik set sail with his family to an island 175 miles (280 kilometers) away, which he named Greenland.

When Erik eventually returned to Iceland, he convinced hundreds of people to join him in Greenland. Twenty-five ships sailed from Iceland, but it is believed that only 14 arrived safely.

Hereward the Wake (1000s)

Hereward the Wake, which means "Hereward the watchful one," was a rebel leader in eastern England. In 1070, Hereward and his men stole treasure from the Peterborough Abbey to keep it from the king. Hereward then moved to the nearby Isle of Ely, an area surrounded by marshes and waterways.

Hereward was betrayed by some of the local people, who showed the king and his army how to safely cross the waterway to the Isle of Ely. Hereward and some of his band managed to escape from the soldiers. Others were captured and had their hands cut off, or they were killed.

The Murderers of Thomas Becket (1100s) ▶

For years, King Henry II of England complained about the disloyal archbishop of Canterbury, Thomas Becket. Four knights heard Henry's complaints and mistakenly thought that the king wanted Becket dead.

On December 29, 1170, the knights rode to Canterbury Cathedral. They broke down the doors, yelled threats, then stabbed and beheaded the archbishop. As punishment for killing Becket, the Pope sent the four knights on crusade to the Holy Land.

Robin Hood (1200s)

Robin Hood was an outlaw from a series of legends first told in the 1200s. The stories tell of Robin and his band of outlaws robbing the rich and attacking the king's soldiers as they passed through Sherwood Forest.

Over time, the legends changed, and Robin Hood was said to steal from the rich to give to the poor. People have tried to discover if the legends about Robin Hood were based on a real person, but no one is certain.

◀ *After the Middle Ages, new characters were added to legends about Robin Hood, including Maid Marion, the woman Robin Hood loved.*

Glossary

abbey A church used by monks or nuns

abbot The male leader of a monastery

apprentice A person learning a trade by working with someone who is more experienced

archbishop The most powerful of the bishops, or religious leaders in the Catholic Church

architect A person who designs buildings

bailiff A person who managed the lord's land and made sure villagers followed the law

Byzantium The area between Europe and Asia, including present-day Turkey and Greece

Catholic Church The only branch of Christianity for most of the Middle Ages, headed by the Pope

Christian A person who follows the teachings of Jesus Christ.

crusade A war fought by Christians against Muslims to recover the Holy Land, the area where Jesus lived and died

empire A group of countries or territories under one ruler or government

exile To force someone to leave the place where he or she lives

guardian A person who is legally responsible for a young child

inherit To receive money or possessions from someone who died

master An artist of great skill

merchant A person who buys and sells goods

Middle East The region made up of southwestern Asia and northern Africa

Muslim Belonging to the religion of Islam. Muslims believe in one God, called Allah, and follow the teachings of his prophets, the last of whom was Muhammad

noble An important person of the Middle Ages

outlaw A criminal who is banished, or forced to leave his or her community

patron A person who supports or protects another person, an event, or a cause

philosopher A person who seeks wisdom, and tries to answer questions about such things as truth, right and wrong, God, and the meaning of life

pilgrim A person who makes a religious journey to a holy place

plague A disease that kills many people

Pope The leader of the Roman Catholic Church

prophet A person who delivers messages believed to come from God

Purgatory A place where Roman Catholics believe souls go after death to be cleansed of their sins before going to Heaven

social class A person's position in society, often determined by his or her wealth

Viking A member of a seafaring people from present-day Denmark, Norway, and Sweden

vision A dream or picture seen in the mind

Index

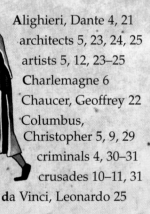
1 2 3 4 5 6 7 8 9 0   Printed in the U.S.A.   2 1 0 9 8 7 6 5